THE IMPACT OF CULTURE: COMMUNICATING WITH IRAN

At no time in history has U.S. involvement in the Middle East been as extensive and complex as it is today. No other region in the world affects U.S. policy and the lives of Americans in such a way as the Middle East, ranging from affecting the lives of families whose loved ones die in Iraq to the price paid for a gallon of gasoline. The Middle East is ethnically and culturally diverse, dynamic, and volatile, which in total can be beyond the comprehension and understanding of many Americans. At the epicenter of this region is the state of Iran, historically known as Persia, which once was an impressive empire that predates the birth of Christianity, Alexander the Great, and the Roman Empire. In addition to occupying the geographic center of this region, Iran wields a high degree of political power throughout and affects geopolitical events well beyond the region. One could argue that although Iran is not the center of gravity with respect to U.S. policy in the region, it plays a decisive role.[1] The role Iran plays exerts influence within the region that is not always congruent with the goals and policies of the United States and its allies. In fact, Iranian internal and external behavior has significant second and third order effects on U.S. regional geopolitical goals and policies.[2]

Iran is located in the geographic center of a region, that struggles with a plethora of geopolitical issues, all of which to some degree directly or potentially affect its future security. To the east is Afghanistan, a fractured state of warlords, drugs, and religious zealots that has a NATO lead coalition seeking to stabilize the government while encouraging the growth of that country's fledging democratic institutions. To the southeast of Iran is a nuclear Pakistan, a fractured political state fueled by internal ethnic and religious strife that also has a fragile peace with nuclear India. To the northeast is Turkmenistan whose communist leaders seem to be following North Korea's example in its effort to isolate themselves from the rest of the world. To the northwest of Iran is Azerbaijan, who is attempting to establish a post Soviet Union style government. Juxtapose to Azerbaijan is Turkey, the only successful Islamic democracy in the region, an active member of NATO and potential future member of the European Union. Looking to west of Iran is Iraq, Iran's historic enemy, and a state where 140 thousand U.S. and allied soldiers remain actively involved in a mission to build an Arabic/Islamic democratic nation. Finally, extending to the southwest are the Straits of Hormuz, where 40% of the West's oil passes through and a myriad of Gulf States, which includes Saudi Arabia, who are long-time regional and religious rivals. In essence, Iran's geographic location does not allow it to exist in a vacuum from its neighbors or the outside world.[3]

With this geopolitical context, the United States has developed numerous strategies to attempt to influence Iran's relationship with its neighbors to achieve U.S. political objectives. However as this paper will examine, historically U.S. strategies to engage Iran have not been effective due to a lack of cultural understanding. To support this premise, this paper will first review U.S. and Iranian interactions over the past fifty years, some of which were good and some not so good. It will then focus on the cultural aspects of Iranian perceptions of themselves, how they view the world and how they communicate with each other, while providing insights into how that translates into Iranian methodologies associated with negotiations. With this broad cultural understanding, the paper will compare how this contrasts with key cultural aspects of

American negotiating techniques and conclude with a number of recommendations on how to effectively engage with Iran from a cultural perspective.

Background: U.S. and Iranian Relations

While America has been involved in the Middle East for over a century, its engagement with Iran began in earnest near the end of World War II. At this point, it is helpful to examine some of the positive and negative aspects of that involvement, which has contributed to mixed U.S. success in influencing Iran over the last decade.

Initially, Iranians viewed American presence favorably, believing it to be a needed-counter balance to British perceived neo-colonialism policy. Toward the end of World War II, U.S. foreign policy tended to look unfavorably upon European colonial aspirations. In fact, some Iranians believed American engagement in Iran was a mechanism to stifle British influence in Iran specifically and within the region generally.[4] With the advent of the Cold War, American foreign policy shifted to actively supporting regimes within the region that were anti-communist. Because of this new policy focus, the U.S. threw its support behind Shah Reza Pahlavi. With the support of the United States, the Shah began a rapid modernization and westernization of Iranian society, which was destined to collide with Iranian society and culture.[5] For example, Iranians started reading American literature, listening to American music and to a lesser extent, watching American television, all of which was viewed negatively by many in Iranian society. Additionally, the Shah embarked on a rapid modernization of the Iranian military, which the United States greatly facilitated with the sale of military equipment and training that proved to be very profitable to U.S industries. During this period, the

American petroleum industry also began to play an active role in interacting with and developing the Iranian petroleum industry.

With the influx of American economic and political capital combined with a more modernized military, Iran became a major petroleum exporter and a political leader within the region backed by a capable military. Under the Sha's leadership, Iran became an important ally to the United States and a stabilizing force within the region. While other Arab countries were directly involved with the Arab/Israeli War, Iran did not. Due to their U.S. relationship, which was not popular with the Iranian people. As the Shah drew closer to the United States, he failed to recognize the second and third order effects of his drive to modernize Iran and his close ties to the United States.[6]

As the Shah pursued his plans of modernizing Iranian society, a number of groups within Iran rejected his policies. The most vocal of these groups was the Shiite clergy, followed by the nationalist and intelligentsia of Iranian society. Because of the Shah's policies, the nationalist within Iranian parliament pressured the Shah to appoint one of their own to Prime Minister, Dr. Mohammed Mossadegh. However, the Shah underestimated Mossadegh's popularity, left-leaning ideology and desire to nationalize the Iranian petroleum industry. The Shah subsequently attempted to remove Mossadegh from power. Because of the visceral backlash brought by the Shah's attempted removal of Mossadegh, the Shah fled Iran, but returned to power several weeks later through a CIA engineered coup.[7]

The CIA led coup had far-reaching effects on American and Iranian relations for the next fifty years. Subsequent to the CIA engineered coup, the Shah established SAVAK, a secret intelligence/police organization used to silence dissent through fear, intimidation, and torture.[8] This agency's actions further contributed to the Shah's alienation with the Mullahs or clergy, which eventually led to his downfall and the rise of Ayatollah Khomeini. It was during this time that the Shah expelled the Ayatollah to Iraq. As the dissent of the people grew, so did repression by the Shah and his regime. Soon a vicious cycle of dissent and repression escalated, and eventually Iran reached a tipping point. In 1979, with pressure growing from within and outside Iran, the Shah abdicated the throne, and Iran became the Islamic Republic of Iran. One could characterize American Iranian relations since 1979 as a roller coaster ride generally on the downward trend beginning with the seizure of the American Embassy in Tehran and culminating with the Iranian support of terrorism and the drive to develop nuclear technologies.[9]

The Islamic Revolution brought significant changes to Iran's policies to include shaping its role within the community of nations. The former polices of the Shah and his drive to modernize Iran came to an abrupt halt. Iran pursued a policy aimed at limiting Western, and more specifically American influence, within Iranian society and the region. Shortly after the Iranian Revolution in 1980, Iraq invaded Iran in an attempt to seize and control the Shatt al Arab Waterway.[10] Iran had no option other than look beyond its borders for weapons and capital to fight the war to achieve its political and economic objectives. Consequently, Iran had to engage the world and not only focus internally. Moreover, while this war ultimately ended in stalemate between Iran and Iraq, Iran explicitly understood the need to shape its political and strategic environment. It is this active geopolitical involvement in sponsoring terrorism and pursuing nuclear technologies while stifling attempts from the United Nations that will now be examined.

<u>Iranian Involvement in Terrorism and Nuclear Capabilities</u>

To achieve its national goals, Iran engaged in state sponsored terrorism as a means to an end. Indeed, one could argue that for Iran, terrorism was a means to project power within the region and to a lesser extent the world. Since the Islamic Revolution in 1979, Iran continues to be an active supporter of terrorism as it armed, trained financed, inspired, organized and otherwise supported numerous terrorist organizations over the past twenty-nine years.[11] In addition to supporting terrorist groups in the Persian Gulf region, Iran supports terrorist and radicals in Lebanon, the Palestinian territories, Bosnia, the Philippines, and elsewhere. Moreover, the U.S government contends that Iran is linked to an array of radical terrorist groups within Iraq in an attempt to destabilize the new Iraqi government and thwart U.S. attempts to establish democratic rule within Iraq and the region.[12] Many view Iranian support of terrorist organizations as an attempt to divert attention away from Iran. For example, to prevent U.S. from directly focusing its political and diplomatic strength on Iran, Iranian support of terrorist organizations such as Hamas and Hezbollah seeks to keep the United States preoccupied with the Arab/Israeli conflict and reduce U.S efforts in enforcing sanctions imposed by the international community related to its pursuit of nuclear technology.[13]

Iran claims it is pursuing nuclear technologies for peaceful purposes; however, some argue the reason for pursuing nuclear technologies is chiefly military. The nuclear polices of Iran have remained consistent over the last three decades even though the national leadership change. Iran pursues nuclear weapons technology for three basic reasons: to deter and if necessary defeat regional adversaries, to establish a leadership position in the region, and to deter global intervention by global powers in Iranian or

Middle-Eastern affairs.[14] The geopolitical reasons for Iranian nuclear pursuit may not be clear as just explained. For example, some contend the real reason is the ability to deter Israel.[15] Although Iran has not fought a war with Israel, there is a deep paranoia with respect to Israeli intentions. It is worth mentioning that to a lesser extent, Iran perceives Egypt, Saudi Arabia, and Turkey as potential adversaries. Some believe that by acquiring nuclear weapons, Iran could easily influence/intimidate other gulf states such as Saudi Arabia or Egypt into accepting Iranian primacy or consider Iranian demands over those of the U.S. or other Western Nations.[16]

Iran's fear of interference in the region derives from past Western perceptions as well as actions taken because of Iranian development of nuclear technologies, and its support to Hezbollah and to Hamas. Specifically, the Bush administration in the 2006 National Security Strategy stated the United States might face no greater challenge from a single country than from Iran.[17] The United States has continued to express its concerns with Iran's attempts at influence in the internal affairs of Afghanistan and Iraq. With respect to nuclear proliferation, since July 2008 the United States pursued a multi-lateral approach, involving its European allies, to engage Iran and persuade them to halt their nuclear program. The intent of this multi-lateral engagement was to communicate to the world that the pursuit of nuclear weapons technologies by Iran is not a U.S.-Iranian issue; rather it is a global issue.[18] Thus, the United States refused one on one negotiation with Iran and instead opted to approach Iran as a member of the global community. [19] These talks, however, have met with little success in obtaining Iranian concessions as the Iranians contend their use of nuclear technology is for peaceful purposes such as energy, while asserting it is their right to do so. Furthermore, the

Iranians argue that if Pakistan, India, and Israel have nuclear weapons and use nuclear energy, Iran should have the same consideration. In response the U.S. Congress proposed legislation that would penalize companies that had bank transactions or trade with Iran. Moreover in 2006 and 2007, the United Nations proposed three resolutions that banned nuclear weapons-related trade with Iran and froze Iranian assets.[20] The United Nations also passed a number of U.N. Security Council Resolutions aimed at preventing nuclear weapons trade with Iran, freezing Iranian assets, banning the transfer of weapons outside Iran and persuading European governments to curb trade, investment, and credits to Iran.[21]

Failed attempts to pressure Iran to stop its pursuit of nuclear weapons led the U.S. and its allies to use *the carrot and the stick methodology* of negotiations. For example, a number of Western states offered a carrot consisting of technical assistance in constructing light water reactors and other economic incentives for peaceful purposes. Additionally, the European Union as well as the U.S. sought to thaw relations by engaging Iran on other issues such as trade and economics. The stick consisted of a comprehensive list of economic sanctions designed to punish Iran should they continue down this path. The list of sanctions included restriction on credit and loans from Western banks, sanctions on Iranian imports and restrictions on Western corporations seeking to do business or investment with Iran.[22] It is important to note that during this time the Bush administration did not eliminate any military options to force Iranian compliance with U.N. demands.

This brief examination of American involvement with Iran over the last fifty years has met with some wins and some losses. However, the current trend has been on the downhill trend of the roller coaster analogy mentioned earlier. If the United States tries to get the roller coaster moving upward, we must first seek to understand Iranians from a cultural perspective.[23] Hence, the paper will now focus on that cultural perspective and its impact associated with negotiations.

National Self Image: How Iranians See Themselves

Iranian self-image is dichotomous in how they see themselves as a nation and how they fit within that nation. First, Iranians see themselves as the children of the Persian Empire, not Arabs but Persians, which is a difference often overlooked by Westerners.[24] This image is almost Chauvinistic, with respect to how they view others. For example, because of the greatness of the Persian Empire Iranians bristle at the notion of Western culture and technological superiority. Consequently, when engaging Iranians, particularly in negotiations, it is prudent to flatter them with respect to their culture and technological sophistication.

Secondly, Iranians see themselves as Shiite, which can be characterized as victims of an unjust world. In terms of being Shiite, Iranians have a fatalistic view; they perceive themselves as victims of a world in which the strong always exploit the weak. In addition, Iranian culture places a great deal of emphasis on the Shiite concept of duality of man, the purity of the inner self and the corruption of the external self. The inner self is the center of all that is good and pure in the world. As such, it is the center of humility, compassion, generosity, and trust in God. The external self is worldly, suspicion, cynical, pessimistic and defeatist; those things that reflect a lack of trust in God. Ideally, one should combat the latter traits and be the person in which both the internal and external self are in harmony, by strict obedience to God.[25] Both concepts could pose advantages to those negotiating with Iranians. With respect to the former, one could play on Iranian fears in terms of reaching a negotiated settlement. For example, one could convince the Iranian interlocutors that no matter what they do they will not achieve a favorable outcome so they should be pragmatic and accept any offer. In the case of the latter, one could appeal to the Iranian inner self, by emphasizing it is God's will to reach a settlement.[26]

How Iranians View the World

Iranians see the world through a prism, which is reflective of the way they see themselves. Mistrust extends to those outside one's family or clan, which creates a feeling or perception projected outwardly toward the rest of the world. The suspicions Iranians harbor toward those outside their inner circle extends to those in power within Iran and outside of Iran, to include government officials. In Iranian culture there is a popular adage that says, "there are many devils in the guise of men, therefore be careful whose hand you put your hand into."[27] This view of the world gives rise to feelings of insecurity, and in all aspects of those things outside of the family gives rise to dissimulation, which is characterized as the hiding of one's real intentions and thoughts. Some contend that Iranian views of self reflect their views of the world. One sociologist assembled a list of traits that characterizes the Iranian middle class as follows: a perception of overall mistrust as men are by nature evil: mistrust of human motivations; mistrust of stability; mistrust of verbal communications by others; the expectation that others will try to manipulate; lack of belief in altruism; exploitation by government of people; and that nothing can change for the better.[28]

Based on these mistrustful notions of leaders and of the world in general, many Iranians see life as a game of chance. In essence, they expect the worst from people and less from individuals in high office. Chance is paramount, and the skill of the individual is vital to the outcome. The individual uses cunning, shrewdness, opportunity and a willingness to take calculated risk to achieve ones end. Nowhere in this equation is the need for teamwork or cooperation seen as a method of mitigating risk to achieve a desired outcome. This is a concept on the opposite end of the spectrum from Western views and in particular American negotiating techniques. For Iranians, teamwork may require the individual to leave his inner circle, placing his trust in those outside his circle. A number of observers assert that over centuries Iranian military failures resulted from mistrust and an inability to work as a team. To illustrate this concept further, some argue that the Iranian criminal underground will never be able to organize in order to perform sophisticated crime similar to that of the mafia, given it would quire trust and cooperation. This cultural trait could be useful in negotiating with Iranian as one could divide and conquer the Iranian negotiators by playing on a lack of teamwork within the team.[29]

A lack of trust in others and an inability to cooperate may be one of the reasons Iranians give so much credence to conspiracy theories, which influence their dealings with world leaders.[30] Iranians tend to view world events through a prism of conspiracy theories, which focus on facts or issues that seem irrelevant to the outsider. To illustrate this perspective, some theories attribute Iran's history and current negative plight to a coalition of Iranian enemies of foreign powers seeking to control Iranian wealth and limit its influence within the region. Iranians believe its enemies conspire through secret organizations and intelligence services, such as CIA and Mossad, to achieve their subversive aims. Iranian schools teach these theories; while many to include academia accepts these theories as truth. For example, some have claimed that the United States and the Israeli intelligence service Mossad established the Iranian intelligence service SAVAK to oppress Iranian citizens. According to many Iranians, since the Peloponnesian War global forces strived to destroy Iranian spirituality and political dominance. The tools of these conspiracies run the gamut from Zionism to Freemasonry and even include the Shiite Ulma, which supposedly returned to power in order exert control over the daily lives of Iranians. Typically, the theories follow two genres of thought; first are those conspiracies fomented by former colonial powers such as Great Britain to include the United States, and secondly conspiracies fanned by unknown hostile global forces or international movements. [31]

Inter-Personal Communications and Negotiations

To understand the techniques and methodologies Iranians use during negotiations, one must understand how culture affects language. In 1976, Edward Hall proposed categorizing culture as either "high context" or "low context."[32] Hall developed this paradigm after observing Asians associated with high context and Westerners to include Americans associated with low context. In the high context terms of communication, this culture is highly language oriented, but it is characterized by linguistic ambiguity and thus dependent on extra-linguistic devices in order to communicate the true meaning. These languages, commonly referred to as shame languages, attempt to hide outward appearances, personal standing, and reputation assume a preeminent role in communications. Conversely, American language, which is

12

low end, does not require additional linguistic devices, and it is described by some as "WYSIWYG," ("what you see, is what you get").[33]

This model is important in understanding Iranian high context communication techniques, which are intentionally ambiguous. Iranian culture believes its language is the heart and soul of Iranian national identity. Everyday Persians employ circuitous and flowery language, which is opaque in nature. The ability to engage in clever discourse is a highly respected trait among many Iranians. Known as zerangi, it involves deliberately misleading adversaries to erroneous interpretations of one's own actions, while determining an adversary's true intention.[34] The discourse is circuitous and ill defined, full of metaphors and misdirects, as it is the task of the listener to decode the speaker's true meaning. Iranians see no need for candor or frankness during discourse. In fact, some in Iranian culture perceive candor as politically incorrect and of no value. The belief among Iranians that the other party will attempt to use zerangi contributes to the overall feelings of mistrust. Indeed, some contend that Iranians are ambiguous in order to protect their pure inner being from the corrupt outer world. It is important to understand that this concept is alien to low end American cultural discourse, in which frankness and directness are very much appreciated and desired during any discussion.[35]

Iranian political culture admires the clever use of ambiguity during negotiations and expects it from foreign political leaders as well. This is very different from American culture in which truth and credibility are paramount. Historically, Iranians make promises through official channels, which they do not keep once they achieve their political objectives. Iranians do not perceive these actions negatively as an Iranian adage states: "A lie that brings benefit is preferable to a truth which causes damage."[36]

The way Iranians communicate among themselves or within their society reflects the way they conduct political and business negotiations. In political negotiation with Iranian authorities, no one person or member of a team has the power to make decisions even with respect to the most trivial matters. This is particularly true when Iranians are dealing with "enemies of the regime" such as the United States, Israel, or other Western powers. As discussed earlier, suspicions run deep within Iranian society and conspiracies abound especially concerning Western nations negotiating teams, in this respect, act as reconnaissance elements that collect data and information, which is later disseminated and discussed. This process differs from Western culture in which empowered interlocutors typically negotiate on behalf of the individuals sending them. In fact, Iranian fear and mistrust extends within the negotiating team itself. The Iranian obsession for collective decision-making leads to constant note sending from negotiators to higher authorities. Official interpreters read these notes aloud to all members of the team, given that the team members do not trust each other. The teams, it is interesting to note, come from a cross sections of Iranian culture, and they may have representation from the Bazzari (business class), the Mullahs, or even the Revolutionary Guard Forces.[37]

As a part of negotiation preparations, Iranian negotiators make extensive use of back channels. There are two reasons Iranians utilize back channel contacts: the first is to minimize public scrutiny of the negotiations; and the second is to identify weaknesses and positions or fractures within the opposing team.[38] Initially Iranians will enter into detailed negotiations in an attempt to gain insight with respect to their opponent. Some argue that this technique reflects a cultural trait, which is designed to elevate the stature of the negotiator among his peers. These issues in many cases spring from tangents, which have nothing to do with the real meat of the original negotiations, but they become the focus of the negotiations. The non-Iranian side then finds that it must negotiate back to the original issue, which it has done so at a price.[39]

Iranian cultural uses time to affect the length, goals, and desired outcomes of negotiations.[40] During the negotiation process, Iranians perceive themselves as the underdog or David facing Goliath, a concept closely tied to the Shiite belief in being the oppressed or exploited masses of the Moslem world. Therefore, Iranians intentionally attempt to draw out negotiations by shifting focus from real issues to ancillary issues unrelated to the negotiations. The intent of this tactic is to buy time in order to achieve a more favorable outcome, hoping the conditions may change. To a western culture and especially American that has a sense of urgency, this can be a very frustrating tactic. A classic example of the use of this tactic occurred during the hostage crisis in Iran in which negotiations lasted over a year. During this crisis, Iranians regularly introduced new issues unrelated to the release of the hostages such as Israel or the Palestinian issue. Moreover, the tactic facilitated the Iranian cultural trait of decision by consensus, which gave the Iranians time to collaborate on key decisions. In addition to introducing unrelated issues, Iranians typically asked for delays in negotiations of several days with the hope that over time conditions would change in their favor. Typically, they asked for one-day extensions, which in actuality resulted in a two to three day delay.[41]

The propensity of Iranians to delay negotiations and create time as a constraining factor contributes to the opaque nature of their style. Many have noted that while Iranians typically come well prepared to negotiate, they shy away from specific details and facts. This negotiating tactic achieves two goals: first, it draws out the length of the negotiations and secondly it confuses counterparts, which again draws out the length of the negotiations. By extending negotiations, some would say that the Iranians accept risk with the hope that conditions will improve in their favor with time. As such, Iranians attempt to mitigate risk through obfuscation and steering the negotiations away from the real issues at hand. In fact, they will look for issues that they believe will put their opponents at risk and widen the scope of the negotiations. An example of this tactic comes from a 2003 Iranian attempt to widen the scope of talks concerning their nuclear development to include their support of Hezbollah in South Lebanon.[42] The intent was using Hezbollah as a bargaining chip. Should any of these tactics fail to achieve the desired goal, Iranians may resort to implausible deniability where they deny facts even in the light of irrefutable evidence. The tactic involves waiting to see what will eventually happen and what issue an opponent will make of it. Finally, after concluding negotiations, Iranians will attempt to make last minute changes or revisit agreed upon terms.[43]

This discussion of time also requires mentioning that Iranian negotiations are very short term focused with respect to the eventual impact of the outcome and do not see building long-term relationships or trust as an outcome of the negotiations.[44] With respect to time, they are very different from Americans. In the U.S., there is recognition of trust building that result from making good faith concessions.[45] Again, Iranian culture views the world as mistrustful. One diplomat described the Iranian sentiment towards trust building as such, "Favors are only grudgingly bestowed, and then just to the extent that a tangible quid pro quo is immediately perceptible. Forget about assistance proffered last year or even last week. What can be offered today?"[46]

American Cultural Traits in Negotiations

American cultural traits in negotiations reflect experiences gained from the history of American westward expansion. Americans approach negotiations based on learned traits that were reminiscent of the Eighteenth and Nineteenth Century westward migration of people from the eastern United States. The westward expansion of America was an opportunity for the disenfranchised to attain large tracts of land and wealth. Profits and rewards went to those whom moved the quickest and demonstrated the most ruthless characteristics. Individuals staked claims, mined, cleared, or farmed, and without class distinction, the prize went to the most resourceful and those willing to take the greatest risk.[47] In some respect, this pioneer spirit replicated the spirit of those that also took great risk when migrating to America from Europe.

Americans, although seen by many as ruthless negotiators, at the same time they are also seen as very straight forward with respect to their dealings.[48] American business/negotiating philosophy is very simple; make as much money or profit as you can in the shortest amount of time. Americans, like the rugged individuals that settled the West, do not mind going it alone and negotiators are empowered to make decisions on behalf of those they represent. American negotiators are also very upfront about the expectations they bring to the negotiating table. They are very quick to put their proposals forward, expecting a counter proposal just as quickly. Indeed, if the other side ignores their offers and does not respond in a timely manner to their proposals, American negotiators can be blunt and offensive. Americans are so preoccupied with speed such that if there is an agreement in principle, most American negotiators seal the deal with a handshake and then work the details of the agreement. However, they are very thorough with respect to the details of the agreement, and they will hold the other party to the last detail to include threatening legal actions should they deviate from the settlement.[49]

In contrast to the American style just described, Iranians are patient, deliberate, and intent on being ambiguous. To many Iranians, an offer at a negotiation table is something to discuss among the members of the team in a very deliberate process. The negotiating team then refers the matter to a higher authority empowered to make a decision. This is a very time consuming process, which can frustrate American negotiators seeking the best alternative to a negotiated agreement.

Recommendations Towards Engagement

With this discussion of historical rollercoaster trends in our past engagements with Iran and cultural considerations of both Iran and the United States with respect to negotiations, there are four broad recommendations to more effectively engage Iran. These recommendations center on the strategic communication efforts, pragmatic attitude, concessions, and geopolitical respect.

The first recommendation concerns Iran's high context culture where ambiguous statements from the U.S. have the propensity to create serious threats. It is important to note that in a high context culture, it is not what you say but how you say it and to some extent where you say it. When a high context culture interacts with a low context culture, there is no clear line of how communication should occur. Therefore, U.S. leaders must articulate their strategic message to Iran in a way that minimizes the possibilities for open-ended interpretation. As in the case with the Iranian nuclear issue, the United States in its strategic communication stated that it would not remove any option from preventing Iranian acquisition of nuclear technologies.[50] Within their high cultural context, Iranians interpreted this as U.S. military action to stop Iran's peaceful pursuit of nuclear technologies. As words are very important, their choice is critically important in terms of strategic communications. Another way this could have been said is, the U.S. is profoundly concerned with Iran's pursuit of nuclear technologies and will explore a number of options to facilitate its peaceful pursuit of these technologies. In this sense, the U.S. would have been more culturally sensitive to its choice of words in strategic communications. Furthermore, if the U.S. were to convey this military option, the best culturally sensitive way would have been a back channel message.

The second recommendation refers to embracing the simple concept that culture complicates everything. Consequently, the U.S. must adopt a pragmatic attitude and accept there are no "cookie cutter" solutions to the issues that separate Iran and the United States. Rather, the United States must creatively and aggressively explore areas for common ground if such exists. The United States must assume that Iran will not enter into discussion with the intent of seeking the best alternative to a negotiated agreement (BATNA). Iran will purposefully keep the negotiations ambiguous and opaque all the while attempting to introduce unrelated issues to the negotiations. The challenge for the United States is not to focus on the final settlement or BATNA but rather to be patient with the overall process. As discussed earlier, American culture

19

looks for immediate results as speed and high pay off is the goal. It is critical that the United States leaders do not become frustrated during the process but remain focused with a clear understanding of the Iranian process and strategy.

The third recommendation involves the concept that Iran will always seek an immediate reward or concession as a part of any negotiation. There is no confidence building or trust building in Iranian culture, and Iranian suspicions of U.S. intentions run deep. Consequently, future negotiations will have to include some form of concession in order to obtain Iranian cultural buy in. For example, if the United States wants to engage Iran with respect to Iraq, then it would be productive if the U.S. recognized the long-standing security concerns that exist between the two countries and agree to address those concerns.

The last recommendation addresses the need for the U.S. to recognize Iranian political, technological, and cultural contributions within the region if it desires to engage in a meaningful dialogue. Within this dialogue, the United States would like to ensure that Iran does not become the regional power, but a respected nation. Moreover, by convincing Iran that they are a respected nation, this may embolden them to feel less threatened by its neighbors. As a result, Iran could be less involved in the internal affairs of Iraq, Afghanistan and the Palestinian cause.

Conclusion

Within the past decade United States involvement in the Middle East increased along with our interaction with Iran, a country which seeks to play a dominate role within the region and whose interests at times conflict with U.S. interests. The United States struggled in its attempt to engage Iran through a number of venues and players with limited success. To better engage Iran requires a cultural appreciation of both nations combined with a historical perspective of the relationship between the U.S. and Iran over the last fifty years that emphasizes recent Iranian involvement in support of terrorism and their drive to acquire nuclear weapons. These last two issues dominate today's geopolitical agenda. They can be better addressed by having a cultural understanding of how both Iranians and the United States communicate and negotiate to bridge differences. With this understanding of key cultural aspects, senior U.S. decision makers should embrace the insights behind the four broad recommendations discussed in this paper on ways to better strategically negotiate and communicate with Iran to achieve our nation's strategic interests.

Endnotes

[1] The center of gravity according to Clausewitz is the hub of all power, which everything moves and depends. Iranian actions affect states such as Afghanistan, Iraq, Saudi Arabia, and Israel, all key players in the region.

[2] *U.S. Department of State Home Page*, http://www.state.gove (accessed December 15, 2008)

[3] Houman A. Sadri, "Surrounded: Seeing the World from Iran's Point of View," *Military Review*, (July-August): 2007, 13. The wide-ranging description of Iran's neighbors comes from this article.

[4] Ibid., 16

[5] Kenneth Katzman, *CRS Report for Congress, Iran: U.S. Concerns and Policy Responses*,(Washington, DC: Library of Congress, Congressional Research Service October 2008), 1

[6] Chris Quillen, "Iranian Nuclear Weapons Policy: Past Present and Possible Future," *Middle East Journal of International Relations*. 6, No 2, June 2002, http://meria.idc.ac.il/journal/2002/issue2/jv6n2a2.html (accessed December 20, 2008)

[7] Stephen Kinzer, *All the Shah's Men: An American Coup and the Roots of Middle East Terror* (Hoboken, NJ: John Wiley and Sons, 2007), 1-17

[8] Nikki R. Keddie and Yann Richar, *Modern Iran: Roots and Results of Revolutions* (New Haven, CT: Yale University Press, 2006), 134

[9] Helen Chapin Metz, ed. "Iran: A Country Study". Washington GPO for the Library of Congress, 1987, http://countrystudies.us/iran/17.html (accessed December 28, 2008)

[10] Houman A. Sadri, "Surrounded: Seeing the World from Iran's Point of View," *Military Review*, (July-August 2007): 18

[11] Katzman, *CRS Report for Congress, Iran: U.S. Concerns and Policy Responses* 27-35

[12] Ibid., 31

[13] Judith S. Yaphe, "Challenges to Persian Gulf Security: How Should the United States Respond?," *Strategic Forum* No. 237 (November 2008) 1

[14] Quillen, "Iranian Nuclear Weapons Policy: Past Present and Possible Future," 1-9

[15] News articles published in the 1990's and early 2000's which former Iranian presidents made reference to the number of nuclear bombs it would take to destroy Israel.

[16] Quillen, "Iranian Nuclear Weapons Policy: Past Present and Possible Future," 2

[17] George W. Bush, *The National Security Strategy of the United States of America* (Washington DC: The White House, March 2006), 20

[18] Katzman, *CRS Report for Congress, Iran: U.S. Concerns and Policy Responses* 36-56

[19] A recent article published in February of 2009 indicates the Obama Administration will consider unilateral discussions with Iran.

[20] Katzman, *CRS Report for Congress, Iran: U.S. Concerns and Policy Responses* 51-58

[21] Ibid., 42

[22] Ibid., 62

[23] Paul Sullivan, "US-Iran Relations since 9-11: A Monologue of Civilizations," *Alternatives: A Turkish Journal of International Relations* 1, no. 2 (Summer 2002): 178-183

[24] Personal experience from working with Iranian and Arabs from 1997-1998 in Kuwait and 2006-2008 during OIF

[25] Shmuel Bar, *Iran: Self-images and Negotiating Behavior*, Conference Report (Tel Aviv: Institute for Policy and Strategy, Interdisciplinary Center Herzliya Lauder School of Government, Diplomacy and Strategy, 2004), 5-6, http://www.herzliyaconference.org. Uploads/2614Iranianself.pdf (accessed December 15, 2008)

[26] Bar, *Iran: Culture Values, Self-images and Negotiating Behavior* 5-6

[27] Andrew Westwood, "The Politics of Distrust in Iran," *Annals of the American Academy of Political Sciences* no. 8, (March 1965) 358

[28] Raymond D. Gastil, "Middle Class Impediments to Iranian Modernization," *Public Opinion Quarterly* 22, no. 3 1958: 325-329

[29] Bar, *Iran: Culture Values, Self-images and Negotiating Behavior* 12-14

[30] Ibid.

[31] Personal experiences and discussions with Iranians that believe the world monetary system is controlled by Jews and Freemasons who are agents of the Jews and Israel

[32] Edward T. Hall, *Beyond Cultures*, (New York: Anchor Press-Doubleday, 1976), 5-6

[33] Ibid., 6

[34] Ibid., 1-6

[35] Ibid., 7

[36] Bar, *Iran: Culture Values, Self-images and Negotiating Behavior* 37

[37] Ibid., 37-38

[38] Ibid., 39

[39] Ibid., 40-42

[40] In 2007, Ryan Crocker, the U.S. Ambassador to Iraq stated during a press brief at the American Embassy in Iraq in which he said he did not want to hold talks with the Iranians until an agenda was set. He referred to the Iranian proclivity to draw out discussions over time with no purpose.

[41] Bar, *Iran: Culture Values, Self-images and Negotiating Behavior* 40

[42] Ibid., 42

[43] Richard D. Lewis, *When Cultures Collide*. (Boston: Nicholas Brealy, 1996), 398

[44] Bar, *Iran: Culture Values, Self-images and Negotiating Behavior* 42

[45] Lewis, *When Cultures Collide*. (Boston: Nicholas Brealy, 1996), 180-181

[46] This was my personal experience while working with Iranians in Kuwait from 1997 to 1998 while assigned to the U.S. Embassy. There is very little if any trust in business dealings or any other dealings for that matter. Friendship and trust does not exist in the same way as it does in U.S. culture.

[47] Lewis, *When Cultures Collide*. (Boston: Nicholas Brealy, 1996), 179

[48] Ibid

[49] Ibid., 180

[50] Katzman, *CRS Report for Congress, Iran: U.S. Concerns and Policy Responses* 37-38